Pashto Language

Teach Yourself Pashto Alphabet

By Babur Abbas

CONTENTS

Pashto Alphabet

There are forty five letters in the Pashto Language. They are as under in the first column and second column denotes the letter sound. Third column shows how each letter is pronounced in a word. In order to master the Pashto alphabet first work on memorizing and recognizing the letters, then our tests will help you distinguish each letter in words. Finally, we'll practice reading whole words together using a rigorous collection of exercises. Let's start with the alphabet first.

Pashto Alphabets	Letter Name	Letter Symbol
ۀ / ٔ	*Hamza*	*A*
آ	*With upper symbol is it called Alif mad aa*	/aa/ (à)
ا	*This without symbol and called Alif*	/a/ in the beginning but /aa/ (à) in the middle or end
ب	*Bay*	/b/
پ	*Pay*	/p/
ت	*Tay*	/t/

بْ	Tay	/t/ (t̪)
ث	Say	/s/
ج	jeem	/j/
چ	Chay	č /ch/
ح	Hay	/h/
خ	Khay	/kh/
خْ	tzay	/tz/ (x Ĵ)
خ̈	Tsay	/ts/ (c)
د	Daal	/d/

ﺩ	Daal	/d/
ﺫ	Zaal	/z/
ﺭ	Ray	/r/
ﮌ	Ray	/r/ (ṛ)
ﺯ	Zay	/z/
ﮊ	Zhay	/zh/
ﮋ	Żhay also called Ghay	/żh /g / (ẑ)
ﺱ	Seen	/s/
ﺵ	Sheen	/sh/

بٚ	It is three regional variations as *Šheen/Kheen/xeen*	/Šh/
ص	*Swaad*	/s/ (ṣ)
ض	*dzwat*	/z/ (d)
ط	*Tway*	/t/
ظ	*Zway*	/z/
ع	*Aeen*	/a'/
غ	*Ghain*	/gh/
ف	*Fay*	/f/
ق	*qaaf*	/q/

ک	kaaf	/k/
گ	gaaf	/g/
ل	Laam	/l/
م	Meem	/m/
ن	Noon	/n/
ڼ	Ṇoon	/Ṇ/
و	wao	/w/ when it is consonant and /o/ or /u/ when it is vowel
ه	hay	/h/
ی	yay	/ay/ it is always used at the end of words

ي	yay	/y/, when it is used as a consonant /i/ and when it is used as a vowel
ې	yay	/e/ is used in the middle and at the end only
ی	yay	/αy/ (ai) is used at the end of words only (for for feminine)
ئ	Yay	/αy/ (ai), used at the end of words only (for imperative)

Alphabet Tests

Test No. 1

Pashto Alphabets	ا 1	ب 2	پ 3	ت 4	ټ 5	ث 6	ج 7
Letter Name	Tay 5	Say 6	Jeem	Alif	Pay	Tay	Bay

Test No. 2

Pashto Alphabets	چ 1	ح 2	خ 3	څ 4	ځ 5	د 6	ډ 7

6

Letter Name	Daal	Tsay	Daal	Chay	tzay	Hay	Khay
	6	5	ح	1	4	2	3

Test No. 3

Pashto Alphabets	ذ	ر	ﻢ	ز	ژ	ي	س
	1	2	3	4	5	6	7
Letter Name	Seen 7	Zhay 5	Žhay also called Ghay 6	Zaal 1	Ray 2	Zay 4	Ray 3

Test No. 4

Pashto Alphabets	ش	ښ	ص	ض	ط	ظ	ع
	1	2	3	4	5	6	7
Letter Name	Swaad 3	Tway 5	Aeen 7	Zway 6	Šheen/ Kheen/ xeen 2	Sheen 1	dzwat 4

Test No. 5

Pashto Alphabets	غ	ف	ق	ك	گ	ل	م
	1	2	3	4	5	6	7
Letter Name	Kaaf 4	Meem 7	Gaaf 5	Ghain 1	Laam 6	Fay 2	qaaf 3

Test No. 6

Pashto Alphabets	ن	نب	و	ه	ي	ي
	1	2	3	4	5	6
Letter Name	Wao	Yay	Yay	Noon	Hay	Noon
	3	6	5	1	4	2

8

Application With Words

Pashto Alphabets	Words in Pashto	Meaning in Roman Urdu/English	Transliteration
ـٔ / ۀ	بنئیل پیٔ لیشل لوئے ویشتل دپاره وئیل کوئید نول	To show To milk Bluffing To recommend Engagement To vanish Fell in love	Khayyal Paye-Laishal Loye-Wishtal Dopara-Wail Qoid-Nol Ghaibi-dal Mayani-dal

	غا ئبیدل مئینیدل		
آ	آبی آخرت آرامی آزادول آسانول آغلی آفرین	Blue The next world Quiet To set free To make easy Beautiful Praise	Aabi Aakhirat Aarami Aazadawal Aasanawal Aaghli Aafreen

	ا	اس|ا ام اوښے ابئِ ارتینۀ اسپه استاذ	Horse Mango Brother in Law Grandmother Women Mare Teacher	*Aas* *Aam* *Aokhay* *Aabai* *Arteenay* *Aaspa* *Ustaaz*
	ب	بابا بابوزے	*Old Man* *Fan*	*Baba* *Babozay*

		Old Women	Budai
	بودی	Goat	Beez
	بیز	She Goat	Bza
	بزه	Gardner	Baghwan
	باغوان	King	Badshah
	بادشاه		
پ	پیشو	Cat	Peesho
	پسه	Goat	Psah
	پیش نمے	Dawn	Pesh-namay
	پیغمبر	Prophet	Peghambar
		Before	Pakhwa
		Father	Plara
		Step Father	Plander

	پخوا پلار پلندر		
ت	تل ترقي تباه تخت تجربه توره	*Always* *Develop Progress* *Destroy* *Throne* *Experience* *Sword* *Arrow*	*Tal* *Tarakay* *Tabah* *Takht* *Tajrubah* *Tora* *Teer*

	تیر		
ب	تول		Tol
	تماتر	All	Tamatar
	توپ	Tomato	Toup
	توبنے	Jump	Tukhay
	توکرہ	Cough	Tokra
	توپک	Piece	Topak
	توپي	Gun	Topi
		Cap	
ث	ثلور	Four	Salor
		Equal	Saani

	ثانۍ		
ج	جونګۍ	Camel Calf	Jongai
	جينۍ	Girl	Jeenay
	جولاها	Weavel	Jolaha
	جوند	Youth	Jwand
	جربنه	Assembly of Elders	Jargah
	جمعه	Friday	Jumah
	جرمانه	To Fine	Jarmana Kol

	کول		
چ	چنغله		Changhala
	چاچي	Fiancée	Chachi
	چرګوتے	Aunty	Chargotay
	چرګ	Chick	Charg
	چيلئ	Cock	Cheelai
	چروبني	Lamb	Charogay
	چاپول	Knife	Chapol
		Printing	
ح	حس	Sense	His

	حاجي	Pilgrim	Haji
	حاجنړه	Female Pilgrim	Hajan-ra
	خاپه	Sad	Khapa
	حلوه	Sweet Dish	Halwa
	حرام	Illegal	Haram
	حلال	Legal	Halal
خ	خر		
	خورزه		
	خاوند	Donkey	Khar

	خورئے	Niece	Khurza
	خواخے	Husband	Khawand
	خواند	Nephew	Khoray
	خاندان	Mother in Law	Khwakhay
		Taste	Khwand
		Family	Khanadan
حٔ	حٔناور		
	حٔنانه	Animal	Zanawar
	حٔلمے	Female	Zanana
	حٔوان	Youngman	Zalmay
	حٔامن	Youngman	Zwan
		Son	Zaman

څ	څپلۍ ثابت څلویښت څه څپیر څلور څڅول څنډل	Shoes Structure Forty What Miserable Four Pour Dusting	*Saplay* *Sakht* *Salwaikht* *Sa* *Spair* *Salor* *Sasawal* *Sandal*
د	درے		

	دادا دوبي درزنره ديكل دوچنده دريم	*Three* *Grandfather* *Washer man* *Seamstress* *Push* *Twice* *Third*	*Dray* *Dada* *Dobai* *Darzan-ra* *Deekal* *Dochanda* *Daryam*
ﺑ	ﺪاكتر ﺪم ﺪول	*Doctor*	*Daktar*

	داحے	Drummer	Dam
	دوبول	Drum	Dol
	داران	Firing	Dazay
	دالے	Sinking	Dobowal
		Coward	Daraan
		Group	Dalay
ذ	ذات		
	ذکر		
	ذلیلول		
	ذهن		
	ذائقه	Caste	Zaat
		Recite	Zikar
		Insult	Zaleelawal
		Mind	Zehan
		Taste	Zaika

	ذاتالریه ذلت	Pneumonia Misery	Zatal-reya Zillat
ر	روژه راٸي رپټ راشه رقیبان راختل رنړیدل	Fast Agree Report Come Rival To Arise Clean	Roxa Raazi Rapat Rasha Raqeeban Rakhtal Ranri-dal

هٔ	هرت بت هرانده هرچیدل اخښني هرندیدل هروندول هرومبي	*Lazy* *Plural* *To Shake* *Arm of a Cot* *To be Deceived* *To Cheat* *First*	*Rut-but* *Randa* *Rachidal* *Akhai* *Randidal* *Randowal* *Rumbai*
ز	زوم زمکه	*Son in Law* *Land* *Lion* *Gold Smith* *To Bear* *Aggrieved*	*Zoom* *Zmaka* *Zmaray* *Zargar* *Zaghmal* *Zahri-dal*

	زمرے	More	Zyat
	زرگر		
	زغمل		
	زهيريدل		
	زيات		
ژ	ژمے	Winter	Xamay
	ژارا	Cry	Xara
	ژوندون	Life	Xwandun
	ژار	Purgative	Xaar
		Crying	Xranda
		To be injured	Xoblidal
		Forest	Xakh

	ژراند ژوبليدل ژاخ		
ږ	ږيرهور ږغږغه ږلۍ ږمونځول ږوي ږاخونه	Bearded Bell Hail To comb Witness Teeth	Geerawar Gagh-Gagha Galay Guman.zawal Gawai Ghakhoona

س	سرے سخر سنډا سخے سپئي سفر سقوط	Man Father in Law Bull Calf Bitch Travel Fall	Saray Skhar Sanda Skhay Spai Safar Sakoot
ش	شپه شاګرد	Night Student Shepherded Poet	Shpa Shagird Shpoon Shayar

	شپون شاعر شبرې شتر مرغ شپه	Night Blind Ostrich Night	*Shabrai* *Shutar Murgh* *Shpa*
بښ	بناپېرک بنکلے وېښنې بنار	Bat Beautiful Awake City Tears Beauty Women	*Khapeerak* *Khwakalay* *Weekhay* *Khaar* *Ookhkay* *Khayast* *Khaza*

	اوبنكي بنايست بنحئه		
ص	صبا صباؤن صداقه صابون صيقل صبر	Tomorrow Dawn Great Love Soap Polish Patience Pectoral	Saba Sabayoon Sadaka Saboon Sekal Sabarnaak Sadrai

	ناک صدري		
ض	ضمانت ضرب ضد ضائع ضرورت ضامن ضبطول	*Bail* *Hit* *Obstinacy* *Waste* *Need* *Guarantor* *To record*	*Zamanat* *Zarab* *Zid* *Zaya* *Zaroorat* *Zamin* *Zabtol*

ط	اطبيبه	Lady Doctor	Tabeeba
	بط	Duck	But
	طاس	Petal	Taas
	طاق	Odd	Taaq
	طوطا	Parrot	Tota
	طرد	Removal	Tard
	طعنه	Taunt	Taana
ظ	ظاهرِي	Outward	Zahri
	ظرفيت	Nature	Zarfeeyat
		Oppression	Zulmat
		Cruelty	Zalam
		Humor	Zarafat
		Humorous	Zareef

	ظلمت		
	ظلم		
	ظرافت		
	ظریف		
	ظاہر	Evident	Zahir
ع	عمل	Act	Amal
	عزت	Respect	Izzat
	علاج	Medication	Ilaaj
	عرصے	Period	Arsay
		Love	Aashiq
		Family	Ayaal
		Humbleness	Ijz

	عاشق عيال عجز		
غ	غوا غوئے غلطي غبن غائبيدل غلط	Cow Bull Mistake Plunder Disappear Wrong Dirty	Ghwa Ghway Ghaltai Ghaban Ghaibeedal Ghalat Ghaleez

	غليظ		
ف	فدرالي	Federal	Fidraali
	فحاشي	Immorality	Fahashi
	فراق	Separation	Firaaq
	فردي	Individual	Fardi
	فرش	Floor	Farash
	فرصت	Leisure	Fursat
	فسخ كول	To Cancel	Fasakh-kol
ق	قاضي	Judge	Qaazi
		Capable of	Qabil

	قابل قهر قياس قمري قبيله قتل	Anger Guess Nightingale Tribe Murder	Qehar Qayas Qamri Qabeela Qatal
ک	كوند كوترے كنزلے	Widower Puppy Abuse Year House Collyrium Begging Bowl	Khwand Kutray Kanzalay Kaal Kor Kajal Kachkol

	كال كور كجل كچكول		
ک	گد گيدر گنرل گدورے گل	Ram Jackal Taking care Lamb Flower Guinea Zoroastrian	Gadd Geedar Ganr-al Gadooray Gwal Gyana Gabar

	كيانا كبر		
ل	ليكه لكئ لونړه لكيره ليونئے لكيا لبدر	Write Tail Daughters Line Mad Busy Ugly	Leka Lakai Lunray Lakeera Lewanay Lagya Labdar

م	مادینه میرمنه مانړګے ملګرے مینه مکنه موظف	Female Wife Sailor Friend Love Window Ordered	Madeena Mairmana Manr-gay Malgaray Meena Magna Mozaf
ن	نائي نارینه	Barber Male Grandmother Squeezing Ninety Trifling	Nayyi Nareena Nya Nachorawal Naway Nagsay

	نيا	Vegetable	Nabatai
	نچورول		
	نوے		
	نۍسي		
	نباتۍ		
نب		No Word	
و	ورارہ	Nephew	Wrara
		Niece	Wreera
		Brother	Wror
	وريرہ	Sister in Law	Wandyara
		Last	Wrustambal
	ورور	Word	Wayi
		Asleep	Weeda

	وندياره ورستمبال ويي ويده		
٥	هلک هاتي هتنره ها هيبت	Boy Elephant Female Elephant That Fear Punishment Indigestion	Halak Hathi Hathanra Ha Hebat Heedad Haiza

	هیداد هیزه		
ی		*Only Used at the end*	
ي	یور ییم یبل یتیم یخچال یو	*Wife husband's brother* *Spade* *Barefooted* *Orphan* *Refrigerator* *One* *Chest of Drawers*	*Yor* *Yeem* *Yabal* *Yateem* *Yakhchaal* *Yo* *Yakhdaan*

		يخدان	

Reading Tests Part I.

Test No. 1

Pashto Word	بنئیل	آخرت	ابئي	بابوزے	پیشو
English Meaning	Grandmother	Fan	Cat	To Show	The next world

Test No. 2

Pashto Alphabets	تل	جولاها	چرکوتے	توپ	ثلور
Letter Name	Jump	Chick	Always	Four	Weavel

Test No. 3

Pashto Alphabets	حاجي	حأمن	څه	خواخے	ديكل
Letter Name	Son	Mother in law	Push	What	Pilgrim

Test No. 4

Pashto Alphabets	رپټ	رخچیدل	دول	زوم	ذلیلول
Letter Name	*Drum*	*Son In Law*	*Report*	*To Shake*	*Insult*

Test No. 5

Pashto Alphabets	ژمے	شاگرد	بنار	بریرهور	سپئي
Letter Name	*Bearded*	*Winter*	*Student*	*Bitch*	*City*

Test No. 6

Pashto Alphabets	صبا	طرد	عرصے	ظریف	ضرورت
Letter Name	*Removal*	*Need*	*Tomorrow*	*Period*	*Humorous*

Test No. 7

Pashto Alphabets	غلطي	کنړل	فردي	کچکول	قمري
Letter Name	*Individual*	*Nightingale*	*Begging Bowl*	*Mistake*	*Taking Care of*

Test No. 8

Pashto Alphabets	مکنه	لیونئے وندیاره	هلک	نګسي
Letter Name	*Trifling*	*Window*	*Boy*	*Mad*	*Sister in law*

44

Reading Tests Part II.

Test No. 1

Pashto Word	بنئيل	آخرت	ابئي	بابوزے	پیشو
Transliteration	*Aabai*	*Babozay*	*Peesho*	*Khayyal*	*Aakhirat*

Test No. 2

Pashto Alphabets	تل	جولاها	چرګوټے	ټوپ	ثلور
Letter Name	*Toup*	*Chargootay*	*Tal*	*Salor*	*Jolaha*

Test No. 3

Pashto Alphabets	حاجي	ځامن	څه	خواخے	دیکل
Letter Name	*Zaman*	*Khwakhay*	*Deekal*	*Sa*	*Haaji*

Test No. 4

Pashto Alphabets	رپټ	ړچیدل	ډول	زوم	ذلیلول

Letter Name	Dol	Zoom	Rapat	Racheedal	Zaleelawal

Test No. 5

Pashto Alphabets	ژمے	شاگرد	بنار	بریرهور	سپئي
Letter Name	Geerawar	Xamay	Shagard	Spay	Khaar

Test No. 6

Pashto Alphabets	صبا	طرد	عرصے	ظريف	ضرورت
Letter Name	Tard	Zaroorat	Saba	Arsay	Zareef

Test No. 7

Pashto Alphabets	غلطي	گنرل	فردي	کچکول	قمري
Letter Name	Fardi	Qamrai	Kachkol	Ghaltai	Ghanral

Test No. 8

Pashto Alphabets	مكنه	ليونئے وندياره	هلك	نګسي
Letter Name	*Nagsay*	*Magna*	*Halak*	*Lewanay*	*Wandyara*

Printed in Great Britain
by Amazon